D0945259

Sports Illustrated KIDS

BASEBALL Jokes

by Blake Hoena

illustrated by Daryll Colins

STONE ARCH BOOKS

Sports Illustrated Kids All-Star Jokes
is published by Stone Arch Books, a Capstone imprint
1710 Roe Crest Drive
North Mankato, Minnesota 56003
www.mycapstone.com

Cataloging-in-Publication data is available on
the Library of Congress website.

ISBN: 978-1-4965-5092-7 (library binding)
ISBN: 978-1-4965-5096-5 (eBook pdf)

Summary: SPORTS ILLUSTRATED KIDS presents an all-star collection
of BASEBALL jokes! With laugh-out-loud home runs like "What has
eighteen legs and catches flies? A baseball team!" these colorful joke
books will have BASEBALL fans rolling in the stadium aisles.

Designer: Brann Garvey

Photo Credits:
Sports Illustrated: Al Tielemans, 20, 28, 57, Damian Strohmeyer, 4, John
W. McDonough, 34, 40, Robert Beck, 12, 46

Printed and bound in Canada.
010382F17

CONTENTS

Just a bit inside!

CHAPTER 1

Batty Batters

What animal is best at hitting
a baseball?

A bat.

Which superhero is the best
at playing baseball?

Batman, of course!

How do baseball players
say hello?

They touch base.

Why are baseball games played at night?

Because bats sleep during the day!

Why does it take so long to run from second base to third base?

There's a short stop between them.

Which baseball player is the best at baking cakes?

The batter!

Why can't chickens play baseball?

They only hit fowl balls.

Why did the baseball player shut down his website?

He wasn't getting any hits.

How are professional baseball
players like pancakes?

They both depend on
the batter.

What do you call a baseball player
who is usually on the bench?

The designated sitter!

Why do some baseball players
cry a lot?

Because they always
choke up on the bat.

When do baseball players take their
bats to the library?

When they're ready to
hit the books.

What do baseball players serve their meals on?

Home plates!

What do you get when you cross a
baseball player with a monster?

A double-header.

What position does
Dracula play?

Bat boy!

Why don't matches play baseball?

One strike and they're out.

Why don't baseball bats shower
after a game?

They prefer bat tubs.

Why did the maid bat fourth in
the team's lineup?

Because he was a
cleanup hitter!

Knock, knock.

Who's there?
Phillip.

Phillip who?
Let's Phillip the bases!

When you're losing but your beard is winning...

CHAPTER 2

Punny Pitchers

Did you hear the joke about the fastball?

Forget it — you just missed it.

Which baseball player holds the team's water?

The pitcher!

Why was the pitcher such a brilliant baker?

She knew how to handle the batter.

Why does a pitcher raise one leg
before throwing the ball?

If he raised both legs,
he would fall down!

How can you pitch a winning baseball
game without throwing a ball?

Only throw strikes.

What do you get when you cross
a pitcher with a carpet?

A throw rug.

Why did the baseball batter
go crazy?

The pitcher kept throwing
screwballs.

Why was the pitcher such
a great singer?

He had perfect pitch!

Why did a herd of cows stampede
onto a baseball field?

They were looking for
the bullpen!

Why did the baseball player
go to the car dealer?

He wanted a sales pitch.

What would you get if you crossed a
pitcher with the Invisible Man?

Pitching like no one
has ever seen.

Why did the pitcher spin
himself dizzy?

To get ready for the
whirl series!

Why was the pitcher such a horrible bowler?

She couldn't throw strikes!

Why did the farmer get thrown out
of the baseball game?

He kept throwing
bean balls.

Why did the pitcher go to the doctor
during spring training?

He had baseball fever!

Why did the pitcher marry
her catcher?

Because he was a
great catch.

Why is a pitcher like a GPS?

He always knows where
home is located

CHAPTER 3

Out of Leftfield

Where do baseball players go
to get their uniforms?

New Jersey.

What has eighteen legs and
catches flies?

A baseball team!

Where did the catcher
sit for dinner?

Behind the plate.

Why was there a frog out
in leftfield?

It was catching flies!

Did you hear the joke about
the pop fly?

Never mind — it will just
go over your head.

What did the glove say to
the ball?

"Catch ya later!"

Why can't you take a catcher to
an all-you-can-eat buffet?

He's always blocking the plates.

Why are baseball players
so rich?

Because they play
on diamonds.

Why did the infielder keep a
rubber band in his pocket?

For the seventh-inning
stretch, of course!

Why did the baseball
go to jail?

It got caught.

A man left home, took three
left turns, and then was confronted
by a stranger in a mask.
Who was the stranger?

The catcher!

What's the difference between an
outfielder and a dog?

An outfielder wears a whole
uniform, but a dog only pants!

What is a baseball player's favorite thing about going to the park?

The swings!

Knock, knock.

Who's there?
Harry.

Harry who?
Harry up and round the bases!

Why did the baseball player build her
house on top of a treadmill?

She wanted to make
her home run!

Why did the baseball team draft
a toddler for their infield?

They needed a short stop.

When you finally finish your homework...

CHAPTER 4

Fanatic Fans

What are the last words of
the national anthem?

"Play ball!"

Why is a baseball stadium the
coolest place to be?

There are so many fans!

Where do baseball players wash
their socks?

In the bleach-ers.

Why were the police called
to the baseball game?

Someone was stealing
the bases!

Knock, knock.

Who's there?

José.

José who?

"José can you see, by the
dawn's early light . . ."

What happened when the
baseball fan fell in a hole?

He was dug out.

What's the best kind of
baseball joke?

One that leaves you in stitches!

What do the weather and a
baseball fan have in common?

They can both get foul.

How do baseball players stay
cool during a game?

They stand next to the fans!

FAN #1: All you ever do is think about baseball.

FAN #2: Nuh-uh — you're way off base!

Why did the baserunner tell the camera operator to move?

He wanted to make sure the camera operator captured his best slide.

What is the difference between a baseball fan and a baby?

The baby will stop whining after awhile.

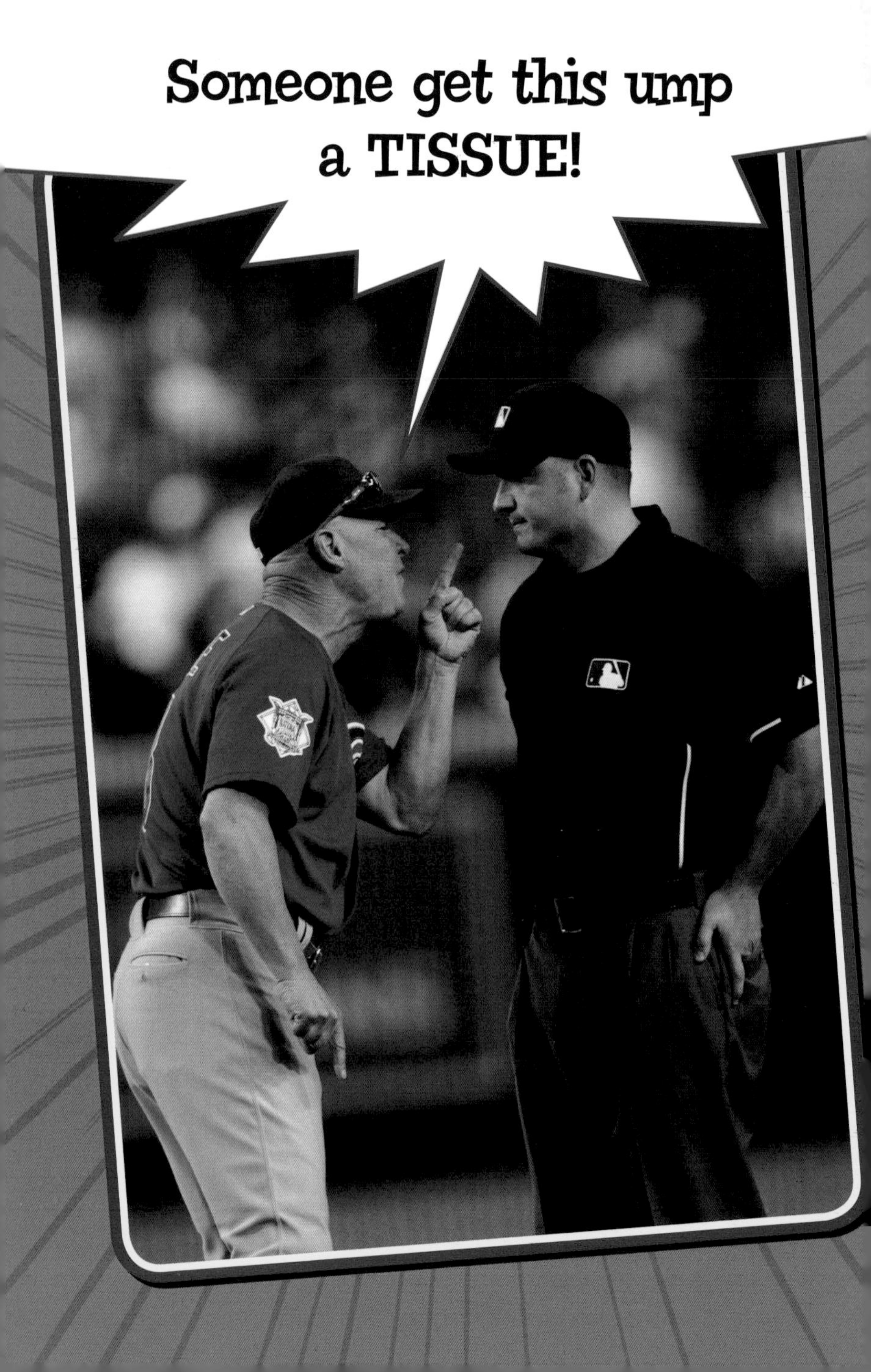
Someone get this ump a TISSUE!

CHAPTER 5

Uppity Umps

Why did the umpire's mom give him dessert?

Because he always cleaned his plate.

What does a coach do if he loses his eyesight?

Becomes an ump.

Where does an umpire learn how to call a game?

The en-strike-lopedia!

Why did the umpire get
fired from his job?

He kept making prank calls!

COACH: Hey, ump! Did you lose your phone?

UMP: No, why do you ask?

COACH: Because you keep missing calls!

What did the umpire do when he caught his kid sneaking in after curfew?

He called him out at home.

What do a horse and an umpire have in common?

They both sleep standing up!

Why did the umpire check the lost and found?

He lost his strike zone.

Why was the umpire late
for the game?

He couldn't even call a cab.

Why did the umpire always
carry a phone book?

In case she needed
to make a call.

What's the difference between
a potato and an umpire?

The potato has eyes!

Kooky Coaches

How many coaches does it take
to change a light bulb?

Who knows — they're too
busy arguing with the ump!

UMP: Why did the baserunner
leave the stadium?

Third Base Coach: Because I
told him to go home!

Why did the pitcher stick his
right hand in a lion's mouth?

The team needed a lefty.

Why was Cinderella so
bad at baseball?

She had a pumpkin
for a coach!

Why did the player leave the
ballpark on a tractor?

The coach demoted him
to the farm team.

Why didn't the coach's son want
help with his hitting?

He wanted to strike out
on his own.

Why did the coach never
eat before a game?

Because she always had
beef with the ump!

How does a coach cure a
late-game headache?

With a pain reliever.

Why is a coach like a chicken?

They both have fowl mouths!

Coach: I'm taking you out of the game.
You're control is off today.

Pitcher: What do you mean?
I haven't missed a bat for
three innings!

Why did the coach buy new
running shoes?

He heard he was in
a pennant race.

Why do baseball coaches
wear uniforms?

Because otherwise they'd
be naked.

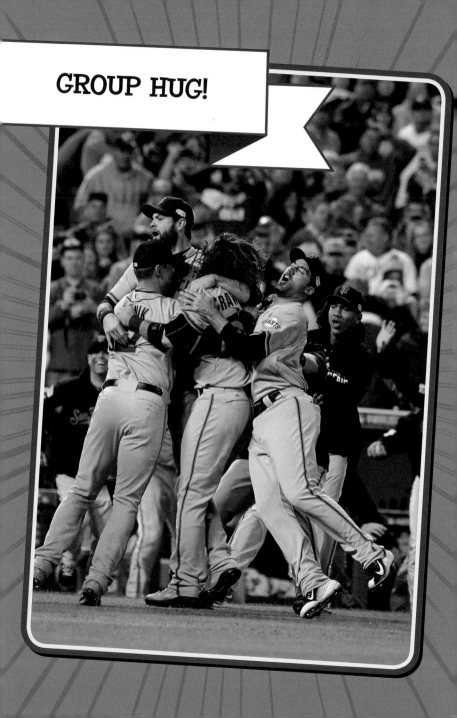

GROUP HUG!

CHAPTER 7

All-Laugh Team

Why is San Francisco's
ballpark so windy?

Because of all the Giant fans.

What did the Angels' coach
catch when he went fishing?

A Mike Trout.

Why did Detroit's baseball team
choose a tiger for their mascot?

Because no one wants to
play against a cheetah!

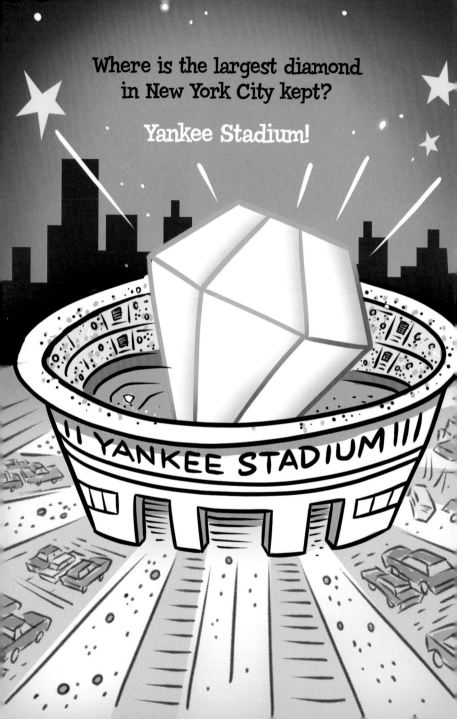

Why did the Los Angeles infielder
jump out of the way of the line drive?

Because he was a Dodger.

Who was the best smelling
baseball player of all-time?

Pete Rose.

Why were Cleveland Indians' jerseys
recalled after the 2016 World Series?

They were considered
a choking hazard!

Why doesn't Iowa have a
professional baseball team?

Because then Minnesota
would want one too.

What do you call an Astros player with a World Series ring?

A thief.

Why was the Cincinatti Reds' Homer Bailey afraid of Baltimore's Mark Trumbo?

Because Trumbo is known for hitting homers.

FAN #1: Why is there a baseball player on top of your fireplace?

FAN #2: That's Mickey Mantle.

What happened when the Blue Jay struck out?

He got so embarrassed he turned Red.

Why did Chicago change its
team name to the White Nylons?

They heard nylons get
lots of runs.

Why is Pittsburgh's baseball
team called the Pirates?

They just arrrrrgh!

What do you call a Tigers team
that hasn't lost a single game?

Purr-fect!

How did the Colorado Rockies
go from first place to last
place so quickly?

The fell off a cliff.

How do the Chicago Cubs
keep their stadium cool?

They use bear conditioning!

What major league team is
always sad?

The Blue Jays.

Why are the Baltimore Orioles
so good at social media?

Because they really
know how to tweet!

Why did the Cardinals
fly south?

Because they were playing
the Miami Marlins.

What do you get when
you cross a tree with a
baseball player?

Babe Root.

Why are the White Sox so loud?

So their feet don't
fall asleep!

What kind of socks do the
Pirates' players wear?

Arrrrrgyle!

Why does Chicago have
two baseball teams?

Because some people
like Sox and others
like bear feet!

Where can you find the best
major league stadium?

On a map!

How to Tell Jokes

1. KNOW the joke.

Make sure you remember the whole joke before you tell it. This sounds like a no-brainer, but most of us have known someone who says, "Oh, this is so funny . . ." Then, when they tell the joke, they can't remember the end. And that's the whole point of a joke — its punch line.

2. SPEAK CLEARLY.

Don't mumble; don't speak too fast or too slow. Just speak like you normally do. You don't have to use a different voice or accent or sound like someone else. (UNLESS that's part of the joke!)

3. LOOK at your audience.

Good eye contact with your listeners will grab their attention.

4. DON'T WORRY about gestures or how to stand or sit when you tell your joke. Remember, telling a joke is basically talking.

5. DON'T LAUGH at your own joke.

Yeah, yeah, I know some comedians break up while they're acting in a sketch or telling a story, but the best rule to follow is not to laugh. If you start to laugh, you might lose the rhythm of your joke or keep yourself from telling the joke clearly. Let your audience laugh. That's their job. Your job is to be the funny one.

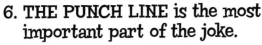

6. THE PUNCH LINE is the most important part of the joke.

It's the climax, the payoff, the main event. A good joke can sound even better if you pause for just a second or two before you deliver the punch line. That tiny pause will make your audience mentally sit up and hold their breath, eager to hear what's coming next.

7. The SETUP is the second most important part of a joke.

That's basically everything you say before you get to the punch line. And that's why you need to be as clear as you can (see 2 above) so that when you finally reach the punch line, it makes sense!

8. YOU CAN GET FUNNIER.

It's easy. Watch other comedians. Listen to other people tell a joke or story. Check out a good comedy show or film. You can pick up some skills simply by seeing how others get their comedy across. You will absorb it! And soon it will come naturally.

9. Last, but not least, telling a joke is all about TIMING.

That means not only getting the biggest impact for your joke, waiting for the right time, giving that extra pause before the punch line — but it also means knowing when NOT to tell a joke. When you're among friends, you can tell when they'd like to hear something funny. But in an unfamiliar setting, get a "sense of the room" first. Are people having a good time? Or is it a more serious event? A joke has the most funny power when it's told in the right setting.

BLAKE HOENA

Blake Hoena grew up in central Wisconsin. In his youth, he wrote stories about robots conquering the moon and trolls lumbering around the woods behind his parents' house. He now lives in St. Paul, Minnesota, with his wife, two kids, a dog, and a couple of cats. Blake continues to make up stories about things like space aliens and superheroes, and he has written more than 70 chapter books, graphic novels, and joke books for children.

DARYLL COLLINS

Daryll Collins is a professional illustrator in the areas of magazine & newspaper illustration, children's books, character design & development, advertising, comic strips, greeting cards, games, and more! His clients range from Sports Illustrated Kids and Boys' Life magazine to McDonald's and the US Postal Service. He currently lives in Kentucky.

Joke Dictionary!

bit (BIT)—a section of a comedy routine

comedian (kuh-MEE-dee-uhn)—an entertainer who makes people laugh

headliner (HED-lye-ner)—the last comedian to perform in a show

improvisation (im-PRAH-vuh-ZAY-shuhn)—a performance that hasn't been planned; "improv" for short

lineup (LINE-uhp)—a list of people who are going to perform in a show

one-liner (WUHN-lye-ner)—a short joke or funny remark

open mike (OH-puhn MIKE)—an event at which anyone can use the microphone to perform for the audience

punch line (PUHNCH line)—the words at the end of a joke that make it funny or surprising

shtick (SHTIK)—a repetitive, comic performance or routine

segue (SEG-way)—a sentence or phrase that leads from one joke or routine to another

stand-up (STAND-uhp)—a stand-up comedian performs while standing alone on stage

timing (TIME-ing)—the use of rhythm and tempo to make the joke funnier

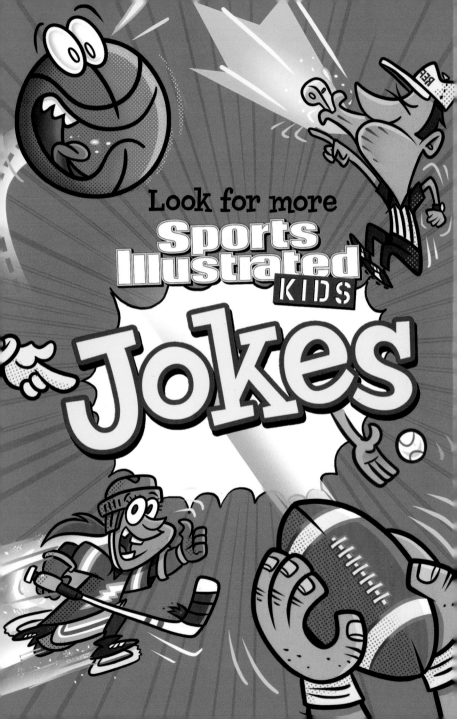

Look for more

Sports Illustrated KID$

Jokes

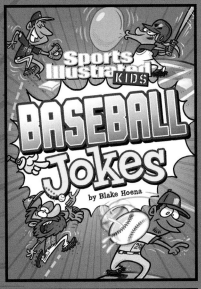

Sports Illustrated KIDS

BASEBALL
Jokes
by Blake Hoena

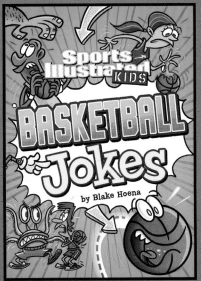

Sports Illustrated KIDS

BASKETBALL
Jokes
by Blake Hoena

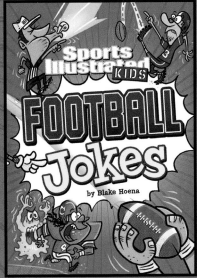

Sports Illustrated KIDS

FOOTBALL
Jokes
by Blake Hoena

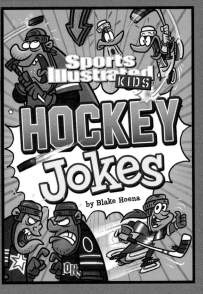

Sports Illustrated KIDS

HOCKEY
Jokes
by Blake Hoena

FACTHOUND

Use FactHound to find Internet sites related to this book.

Visit www.facthound.com

Just type in 9781496550927 and go.

 Check out projects, games and lots more at
www.capstonekids.com